D0119101

World Book's Documenting History

Independence of India and Pakistan

WORLD BOOK

a Scott Fetzer company
Chicago

www.worldbookonline.com

World Book, Inc.
233 N. Michigan Avenue
Chicago, IL 60601
U.S.A.

For information about other World Book publications, visit our website at **http://www.worldbookonline.com** or call **1-800-WORLDBK (967-5325).**

For information about sales to schools and libraries, call **1-800-975-3250 (United States),** or **1-800-837-5365 (Canada).**

Library of Congress Cataloging-in-Publication Data

Independence of India and Pakistan.
       p. cm. -- (World Book's documenting history)
    Summary:"A history of the struggle for independence in India and Pakistan, based on primary source documents and other historical artifacts. Features include period art works and photographs; excerpts from literary works, letters, speeches, broadcasts, and diaries; summary boxes; a timeline; maps; and a list of additional resources"-- Provided by publisher.
    Includes bibliographical references and index.
    ISBN 978-0-7166-1506-4
    1. India--History--Autonomy and independence movements--Sources--Juvenile literature. 2. India--Politics and government--1919-1947--Sources--Juvenile literature. 3. India--History--Partition, 1947--Sources--Juvenile literature. 4. Pakistan--History--Autonomy and independence movements--Sources--Juvenile literature. 5. Pakistan--Politics and government--20th century--Sources--Juvenile literature. I. World Book, Inc.
DS480.45.I44 2011
954.03'5--dc22
                                        2010011909

World Book's Documenting History
Set ISBN 978-0-7166-1498-2
Printed in Malaysia by TWP Sdn Bhd, JohorBahru
2nd printing January 2012

Staff

Executive Committee

President
  Donald D. Keller
Vice President and Editor in Chief
  Paul A. Kobasa
Vice President Marketing/Digital Products
  Sean Klunder
Vice President, Licensing & Business Development
  Richard Flower
Controller
  Yan Chen
Director, Human Resources
  Bev Ecker

Editorial

Associate Director, Supplementary Publications
  Scott Thomas
Senior Editor, Supplementary Publications
  Kristina Vaicikonis

Manager, Contracts & Compliance
(Rights & Permissions)
  Loranne K. Shields
Researcher, Supplementary Publications
  Annie Brodsky
Editorial Researcher
  Jon Wills
Administrative Assistant
  Ethel Matthews

Editorial Administration

Director, Systems and Projects
  Tony Tills
Senior Manager, Publishing Operations
  Timothy Falk
Associate Manager, Publishing Operations
  Audrey Casey

Manufacturing/Production/Graphics and Design

Director
  Carma Fazio
Manufacturing Manager
  Steven K. Hueppchen
Production/Technology Manager
  Anne Fritzinger
Production Specialist
  Curley Hunter
Proofreader
  Emilie Schrage
Manager, Graphics and Design
  Tom Evans
Coordinator, Design Development and Production
  Brenda B. Tropinski
Senior Designer
  Isaiah W. Sheppard, Jr.
Associate Designer
  Matt Carrington

Marketing

Associate Director, School and Library Marketing
  Jennifer Parello

Produced for World Book by
Arcturus Publishing Limited

Writer: Stewart Ross
Editors: Patience Coster, Alex Woolf
Designer: Jane Hawkins

Contents

India and the Europeans

EUROPEAN MERCHANTS, EAGER TO EXCHANGE THEIR MANUFACTURED GOODS for silks and spices, first made direct contact with the people of what is now India in the late 1400's. A Portuguese explorer, Vasco da Gama (1469?-1524), arrived on the Indian *subcontinent* (a large section of a continent with a certain geographical or political independence) in 1498, and Portugal eventually gained control over areas of the western coast. In 1600, Queen Elizabeth I (1533-1603) of England granted a charter to the East India Company to trade with India. The Muslim Mughal Empire that had ruled India since 1526 eventually went into decline, allowing European intruders to compete for power and influence. The British East India Company proved most successful in this competition and, by the mid-1800's, dominated the entire country.

◀ Akbar the Great (1542-1605) was the most impressive of the Mughal emperors—Muslim rulers who controlled much of India from the 1500's to the mid-1800's. When India's Hindu majority sought independence from the United Kingdom in the 1900's, some of them felt they were throwing off 400 years of foreign rule, Mughal as well as British.

▶ Portuguese explorer Vasco da Gama describes in the journal his arrival in the port of Calicut (also called Kozhikode) in May 1498. At this early stage, relations between Indians and Europeans were peaceful and on an equal footing. Only later, as central authority in India collapsed, did the visitors gradually change from traders to invaders.

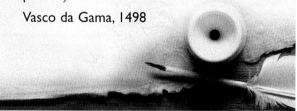

When we arrived at Calicut the king was fifteen leagues away. The captain-major [da Gama] sent two men . . . informing him that an ambassador had arrived from the King of Portugal with letters, and that if he desired it he would take them to where the king then was. The king presented the bearers of this message with much fine cloth. He sent word to the captain-major bidding him welcome, saying that he was about to proceed to Qualecut (Calicut).

Vasco da Gama, 1498

▶ Robert Clive (1725-1774), commander of British East India forces, greets General Mir Jafar after defeating the *nawab* (Mughal governor) of Bengal at the Battle of Plassey on June 23, 1757. The nawab, Siraj-ud-Daulah, tried to force the English out of Bengal. His general, Mir Jafar, plotted with the British to depose Siraj-ud-Daulah. With Mir Jafar installed as the new nawab, Clive became virtual ruler of the state of Bengal, which historians mark as the real beginning of the Raj.

3

4

It would be, therefore, grossly criminal to condemn that sex [women] to death merely from precaution. By *ascribing* [crediting] to them all sorts of improper conduct, you have indeed successfully persuaded the Hindoo community to look down upon them as *contemptible* [deserving of scorn] and *mischievous* [harmful] creatures, whence they have been subjected to constant miseries.

Raja Rammohun Roy, 1820

◀ Indian intellectual Raja Rammohun Roy (1772-1833) argues in an essay published in 1820 against the Hindu practice of *suttee*—burning a widow on her husband's funeral *pyre* (stacked wood upon which a body is burned). Roy was a founder of the Bengal Renaissance, a reform movement that drew on Indian and European ideas. The movement began in the early 1800's and lasted into the 1900's. The founders sought to reform Hindu social and religious practices, including the treatment of women and the *caste system* (a system of social classes in India). Roy, who introduced the word *Hinduism* into English, helped to convince the British colonial government to ban the practice of suttee.

NOW YOU KNOW

- Regular direct contact between India and Europe did not begin until the late 1400's.
- From the 1600's, Europeans took advantage of the decline of the Mughal Empire to extend their power and influence across the country.
- By 1850, the British East India Company was the greatest power in the land. British ideas began to influence Indian thought.

The British Raj

THE EAST INDIA COMPANY WAS ORIGINALLY A TRADING ORGANIZATION. Although it developed its own *civil service* (workers that administered services) and even its own armies, it was hardly suited for ruling a huge country like India. The turning point came in 1857 when the company's Indian soldiers, known as *sepoys*, rebelled. During the rebellion (which ended in 1859), the British Parliament passed the Government of India Act of 1858, which transferred control of much of India from the East India Company to the British government. For the next 90 years, most Indians lived either in states governed by the British or in princely states—that is, states governed by Indian princes, called maharajahs, under British oversight. The system of British governance in India was known as the *Raj*, meaning "rule."

▶ By 1900, the vast majority of India was ruled by the British. The Raj stretched from the Himalayan Mountains in the north to Ceylon (now Sri Lanka) in the south; from the rugged frontier with Afghanistan in the northwest to the long finger of Burma (now Myanmar) in the southeast. Small areas within British India were, however, controlled by other countries—for example, Goa was held by the Portuguese.

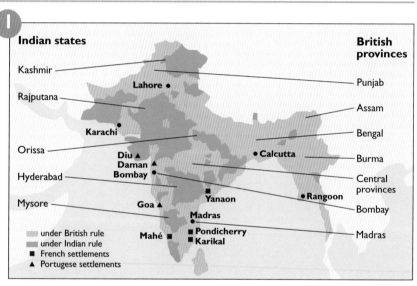

Indian states / **British provinces**

Kashmir
Lahore •
Rajputana
Punjab
Assam
Karachi
Bengal
Orissa
Diu ▲
Calcutta
Burma
Daman ▲
Hyderabad
Bombay •
Central provinces
Mysore
Yanaon ■
Rangoon •
Goa ▲
Bombay
Madras •
Pondicherry ■
under British rule
Mahé ■
Karikal ■
Madras
under Indian rule
■ French settlements
▲ Portugese settlements

The ceremony was most imposing [majestic]. . . . Three tented pavilions [platforms] had been constructed on an open plain. The throne-pavilion in the center was . . . brilliant in hangings and banners of red, blue, and white satin magnificently embroidered [sewn] in gold with appropriate emblems [symbols]. It was hexagonal in shape, and rather more than 200 feet in circumference. In front of this was the pavilion for the Ruling Chiefs and high European officials. . . .

Frederick Sleigh Roberts, 1897

◀ Roberts (1832-1914), eventually Lord Roberts, describes in his journal the spectacular ceremony in Delhi, India, on Jan. 1, 1877, at which Victoria (1837-1901), queen of the United Kingdom of Great Britain and Ireland, was proclaimed empress of India. The queen was not in attendance. She was represented by Robert Bulwer-Lytton, 1st Earl of Lytton, viceroy of India. The attendance of most of India's wealthy and powerful elite signaled their acceptance of their country's position in the British Empire.

◀ Lord Curzon (1859-1925), viceroy of India from 1899-1905, and his wife, Baroness Curzon (1870-1906), show off a tiger killed on a hunt in Hyderabad in 1902. During the Raj, the viceroy, or governor general, was the head of the British administration in India and the representative of the British monarchy.

▶ In "British India," published in *The Atlantic Monthly* in 1857, Charles Hazewell (1814-1883) justifies British rule in India on the grounds that the country had a long tradition of foreign rule. The usual reasoning was that the British brought to India the benefits of good government and improvements in transportation, medicine, and education. Some Christians justified it on the grounds that it introduced Christianity to non-Christians. Many Indians, however, resented foreign rule.

There is nothing like the rule of the English in India to be found in history. . . . The harshest *condemnation* [complaint] that has visited England because of her Indian successes has proceeded from nations who have never been backward in seizing the lands of other nations. [Britain] has been *stigmatized* [disgraced] as a *usurper* [one who takes power by force without the right], and as having destroyed the independence of Indian states. The facts do not warrant these charges. . . . The Moghul dynasty was as foreign to India as the East India Company. . . .

Charles Creighton Hazewell, 1857

NOW YOU KNOW

- In 1858, the British government took over responsibility for the government of India, ruling some states directly and leaving others in the hands of local princes.
- British rule, headed by Queen Victoria, was known as the Raj.
- Many Indians resented British rule.

Roots of Indian Nationalism

B RITISH JUSTIFICATIONS OF THE RAJ AND EVEN THE SUPPORT of more than 560 Indian princely states could not alter the fact that the Raj was built upon *racism* (choosing or preferring one group over another solely because of their race). In 1900, a white minority of some 7,500 people ruled a population of between 250 million and 270 million Indians. All the top positions in India were reserved for the British. Their privileged position rested ultimately on force—a large standing army and police force. There were always Indians, especially among the better educated, who resented British rule. In 1876, this resentment resulted in the founding of the Indian National Association, with developed branches around the subcontinent. Indian *nationalism* (a sense of common belonging and loyalty to a nation) was on the rise.

◀ The Attack on the Peiwar Kotal by the 5th Gurkha Rifles, Afghanistan, December 1878, an oil by Vereker Monteith Hamilton (1856-1931). The painting depicts the "storming of the Peiwar Kotal Pass," an attack by the Gurkha Rifles, a British unit, on Afghan forces in November 1878. The Gurkhas lived in parts of northern India and Nepal. The British admired them as great soldiers. However, British officers were in charge of the Gurkha Rifles. The fact that British officers led all Indian units in the British Army in India fostered resentment.

2

To sum up . . . the British rule has been—morally, a great blessing; politically, peace and order on one hand, blunders on the other. . . . The natives call the British system "Sakar ki Churi," the knife of sugar. That is to say, there is no *oppression* [cruel or unjust treatment], it is all smooth and sweet, but it is the knife. . . . Our great misfortune is that you do not know our wants. When you will know our real wishes, I have not the least doubt that you would do justice. The genius and spirit of the British people is fair play and justice.

Dadabhai Naoroji, 1887

◀ In *Essays, Speeches, Addresses and Writings* (1887), Indian intellectual and political reformer Dadabhai Naoroji (1825-1917) describes what many educated Indians felt: While India benefited from certain aspects of the British Raj, Indians resented living under *alien* (foreign) rule. Naoroji lived in the United Kingdom for a time and was the first Asian Member of Parliament (MP). Naoroji, A.O. Hume, and Dinshaw Edulji Wacha are credited with founding the Indian National Congress.

▶ Speaking to members of the Indian National Congress in 1915, Surendranath Banerjee (1848-1925) suggested that World War I (1914-1918) would lead to "readjustments" that would "set right" the plight of the suppressed people of the world. Banerjee founded the earliest Indian political organization, the Indian National Association, for which he was called Rashtraguru, "teacher of the nation." He was a moderate who favored dialogue and compromise with the British, who called him "Surrender Not Banerjee" for his persistence.

3

The idea of re-adjustment is in the air, not only here in India but all the world over. The heart of the [British] Empire is set upon it . . . . What is this war for? Why are these numerous sufferings endured? Because it is a war of re-adjustment, a war that will set right the claims of minor nationalities.

Surendranath Banerjee, 1915

NOW YOU KNOW

- The British Raj practiced racist policies in that it heavily favored British people over Indians.
- Indian nationalism was on the rise by the late 1800's.
- The first organization to reflect Indian nationalism was the Indian National Association.

The Congress Party

IN 1885, THE FOCUS FOR INDIAN NATIONALISM SHIFTED when 70 representatives—lawyers, teachers, businessmen, and intellectuals—from all of India's British-governed provinces met in Bombay (now Mumbai). They formed a political party, which they named the Indian National Congress (or Congress Party). Within two years, the organization had absorbed the Indian National Association and become a powerful voice for more equal opportunities for Indians in their own land. However, the party was faced with difficult choices: Should it seek full independence from the United Kingdom? What tactics should the Congress Party adopt? Should violence be employed as a tactic? And, most difficult of all, did the party speak for both the Hindu majority (70 percent of the people in India) and Muslim minority (20 percent of the people)?

1

And first suppose that all the Mahomedan [Muslim] electors vote for a Mahomedan member and all Hindu electors for a Hindu member. Now count how many votes the Mahomedan member has and how many the Hindu. It is certain the Hindu member will have four times as many because their population is four times as numerous. ... And how can the Mahomedan guard his interests?

Syed Ahmed Khan, 1887

In a lecture given in Lucknow, India, in 1887, Muslim leader Sir Syed Ahmed Khan (1817-1898) spoke on the attitude that the Muslim community might assume toward the political questions of the day. Khan was worried that Indian democracy would lead to those of his faith being *marginalized* (made less important). Nineteen years later, in 1906, the All-India Muslim League was founded to protect Muslim interests within the Indian nationalist movement.

2

▶ The goals of the National Congress Party crossed cultural differences and traditions, attracting members of Indian's many faiths and customs. The party chairman, Motital Nehru (1861-1931), is seated at the center of the second row. To his right is Bal Gangadhar Tilak (1856-1920). The two men represented the party's main factions: Nehru the moderate and Tilak the militant.

3

At present we are clerks and willing instruments of our own oppression in the hands of an alien government, and that government is ruling over us not by its innate [naturally existing] strength but by keeping us in ignorance and blindness to the perception [knowledge] of this fact.

Bal Gangadhar Tilak, 1907

4

▲ In a 1907 speech before the Congress Party, journalist Bal Gangadhar Tilak (1856-1920) called the British foreign *oppressors* (those who keep others down unjustly) who ruled through enforced ignorance. Leader of the militant wing of the party, Tilak was imprisoned from 1908 to 1914 for defending violent opposition to British rule. His slogan "Swaraj [home rule] is my birthright and I shall have it" inspired millions of Indians.

▶ Sir Muhammed Shah, Aga Khan III (1877-1957) at the fashionable French resort of Deauville in 1925. The stability of the Raj was reinforced by the willingness of the British establishment to welcome aristocratic and royal Indians, such as the Aga Khan, into its midst. Leader of the Shi`ite Ismaili Muslims, the Aga Khan was sometimes described "as British as the British."

NOW YOU KNOW

- Founded in 1885, the Congress Party became the focus for Indian hopes and aspirations.
- Congress Party members disagreed on what tactics to use to gain independence.
- During the Raj, tensions existed between the Hindu majority and the Muslim minority, and in 1906, Indian Muslims formed their political party, the All-India Muslim League.

Bengal and Bloodshed

CONTROL OF THE RAJ GOVERNMENT WAS DIVIDED between a London-based secretary of state for India and the India-based viceroy. The title viceroy means "in the place of the king." The viceroy had great power, though he was expected to consult with locals, British and Indian. Viceroys varied in their level of commitment. Lord Curzon (see also page 7), who served from 1899 to 1905, greatly improved government efficiency. However, his decision to divide the province of Bengal provoked a great wave of nationalism. The Congress Party accused him of trying to undermine the nationalist movement, which was centered in Bengal, by dividing Bengal. Curzon resigned, and Secretary of State John Morley (1838-1923) introduced the Government of India Act of 1909 (Morely-Minto Reforms), which gave well-placed Indians a greater say in their own government.

1

◀ Gilbert John Elliot-Murray-Kynynmound (1845-1914), 4th Earl of Minto, served as Indian viceroy from 1905-1910. Minto, who poses as a king might in this photo, was a great supporter of empire: "We shall fight for the Raj as hard as we have ever fought," he wrote to John Morley, "and if it comes to fighting, we shall win as we have always won."

▶ Indian writer Bankim Chandra Chatterjee (or Chattopadhyay) (1838-1894) wrote "Vande Mataram" in 1876. The poem is a hymn to the Hindu goddess Durga, whom Indians identified as a symbol of Bengal (now an area of northeast India and western Bangladesh). Chatterjee's lines set to music became a rallying cry for the Indian freedom movement. The song became an alternate national anthem to "God Save the Queen," which the British demanded be sung at all public meetings. Muslim Indians objected to Chatterjee's Hindu imagery as *idolatry* (idol worship).

2

Mother, I bow to thee!
Rich with thy hurrying streams,
bright with orchard gleams,
Cool with thy winds of delight,
Dark fields waving Mother of might,
Mother free. . . .

Who hath said thou art weak in thy
   lands
When swords flash out in 70 million
   hands
And 70 million voices roar
Thy dreadful name from shore to
   shore?

The "Vande Mataram"
("Hail to thee, mother," or
"Bow to mother"), India's
national song

3

To them [the English] I would respectfully say: "I admit you are my rulers. It is not necessary to debate the question whether you hold India by the sword or by my consent. I have no objection to your remaining in my country, but although you are the rulers; you will have to remain as servants of the people. . . . You may keep the riches that you have drained away from this land, but you may not drain riches henceforth. . . . We hold the civilization that you support to be the reverse of civilization. We consider our civilization to be far superior to yours.

Mohandas Gandhi, 1909

◀ Writing in 1909, the lawyer Mohandas Gandhi (1869-1948) sets out his views on *Swaraj*—home rule, or self-rule. Rejecting violence, he makes it clear that the British are simply guests in a country whose culture and values are superior to their own. After the Bengal revolt, Indians inspired by the idea of self-rule *boycotted* (refused to buy or use) all things British in favor of Indian-made goods.

4

▶ A recruiting poster for the Indian Army from the Victorian era (during the reign of Queen Victoria, 1837-1901). The image suggests that soldiers in the Indian Army are well-dressed and proud, compared with the peasant with his begging bowl.

NOW YOU KNOW

- The structure of the Raj government included a powerful viceroy.
- Viceroy Curzon's division of Bengal stoked the fires of Indian nationalism.
- The British tried to soothe Indian anger with the Government of India Act of 1909.

World War I

B Y 1914, THE INDIAN NATIONALIST MOVEMENT WAS MADE UP of smaller groups with various identities—groups advocating a violent overthrow of British rule and groups advocating nonviolence; groups with members who were only Hindu, Muslim, or practiced other religious beliefs; and groups demanding immediate independence and those seeking a gradual move towards independence. When World War I (1914-1918) was declared, India rallied behind the United Kingdom. The Indian National Congress and influential Indian leaders believed that their cause would best be served by helping in whatever capacity possible, including sending soldiers and financial aid. However, they expected their sacrifice to be rewarded by *concessions* [privileges granted] toward independence. When their hopes were disappointed, anti-British sentiment grew stronger.

1

This National Congress [party] and the Moslem League met in Lucknow this Christmas in unusual circumstances. . . . Congress [is] under the control of those who have never cooperated with the [British] Government and whose energies are bent on the early *attainment* [gaining] of self-government or Home Rule. . . . During the sessions it was announced that a joint committee of the Congress and the Moslem [Muslim] League had reached complete agreement. . . . The *ascendancy* [rise] of these political forces . . . is a very significant sign of the times.

The Times, Jan. 3, 1917

◀ The editors of *The Times*, a London newspaper, were clearly worried about the political *alliance* (joining of interests), known as the Lucknow Pact, in which the All-India Muslim League joined with the Congress Party to support Britain in World War I. India's Muslims were more reluctant than Hindus to fight for the United Kingdom. It would mean that they would be fighting against fellow Muslims in the Ottoman Empire, a Turkish empire that included much of modern Turkey, Syria, Lebanon, and Israel.

2

▶ Indian soldiers of the Sikh religion defend British-held Egypt against Turkish forces at the Suez Canal in 1915. Sikhism is a religion that began in northwestern India in the 1400's. British generals preferred to use Hindu and Sikh soldiers for operations in the Middle East, as Muslim regiments were reluctant to attack fellow Muslims.

▶ A British officer writes in 1915 of his surprise at the high quality of Indian soldiers fighting alongside him. British military officials slowly recognized this and, in 1917, finally allowed Indians to become officers. Almost 1 million Indian soldiers fought on every front in World War I for the United Kingdom.

We were attached to the Indians. There was one battalion of Gurkhas [from Nepal and northern India], the 1st/39th Garhwalis [from the north of India], the 2nd Leicesters [a British battalion] and ourselves. It was very interesting because you would have expected the Gurkhas and the Garhwalis, who are hillmen, wouldn't have taken to the flat Flanders [a region of Belgium] country with all that mud. But they were very much better than the . . . Punjabis [from the north of India] and Sikhs. They were less frightened.

Captain A. V. L. B. Agius, 1915

◀ The gravestone of an Indian soldier who died in World War I, in a military cemetery in Étaples, France. More than 43,000 Indian troops died in the war.

NOW YOU KNOW

- During World War I, Indian troops fought for the United Kingdom.
- India's Muslim soldiers were reluctant to fight fellow Muslims in the armies of the Ottoman Empire.
- When the British failed to reward India's wartime loyalty with independence, previously splintered nationalist groups united against British rule.

Amritsar Massacre

RATHER THAN REWARD INDIA'S WARTIME SUPPORT, the British government clamped down after the war. In 1919, the British majority on India's Supreme Legislative Council forced through a peacetime extension of strict wartime security measures. The act permitted authorities to imprison suspected terrorists without trial. Resentment mounted, especially in the Punjab, from which half of all India's soldiers had come. By April, the region was in turmoil. The violence climaxed in Amritsar, where on April 10 a mob killed five Europeans. Brigadier General R. E. H. Dyer (1864-1927) arrived with troops on April 11 and banned pubic meetings. On April 13, Dyer ordered troops to fire on an estimated crowd of 20,000 people. In 10 minutes, about 400 Indians were killed, 1,200 were wounded, and Indians had lost their faith in British justice.

▲ A painting of the Amritsar Massacre captures the crowd's helplessness and the pointless cruelty of the shootings. The painting is not, however, accurate in all details: machine guns were not used, for example.

▶ A Congress subcommittee report demonstrates how the Amritsar Massacre—"a calculated piece of inhumanity"—destroyed Indian faith in the British idea of "fair play."

The Jallianwala Bagh [Amritsar] massacre was a calculated piece of *inhumanity* [cruelty] towards utterly innocent and unarmed men, including children, and unparalleled for its ferocity in the history of modern British administration.

from the Congress Party Punjab subcommittee report on the massacre

3

> The crowd was unarmed, except with *bludgeons* [clubs]. It was not attacking anybody or anything. . . . When fire had been opened upon it to disperse it, it tried to run away. . . . Many threw themselves down on the ground, and the fire was then directed on the ground. This was continued for 8 or 10 minutes, and it stopped only when the ammunition had reached the point of exhaustion.
>
> Winston Churchill, 1920

▲ In 1920, Winston Churchill (1874-1965), a future prime minister, reported to the British House of Commons on the Amritsar Massacre. A firm believer in the British Empire, Churchill opposed Indian independence. Nevertheless, he understood how the unnecessary slaughter of some 400 civilians and wounding of another 1,200 Indians had seriously damaged British authority in India.

4

SAVIOUR OF INDIA, OR GUILTY OF AN "ERROR OF JUDGMENT"?

▲ A July 1919 edition of *The Illustrated London News,* discussing the Amritsar Massacre, questions whether Brigadier General Dyer (above) was the "saviour of India" or guilty of a grave "error of judgment." The editors' indecision betrays a great deal about British thought at the time. Elsewhere in the world, his order to attack was thoroughly condemned. Although Dyer was never formally punished, he was forced to resign from the army, a great humiliation.

NOW YOU KNOW

- After World War I, a law was enacted that allowed suspected terrorists to be jailed without being tried in court.
- Hostility to Britain was strongest in the Punjab, where violence on both sides led to the Amritsar Massacre of 1919.
- The massacre convinced many Indians that British rule was not to their benefit.

Reform

EVEN BEFORE THE AMRITSAR MASSACRE, THE BRITISH GOVERNMENT had plans to meet some Indian demands for self-rule while still keeping the country within the British Empire. The Government of India Act of 1919 required that at least three Indians sit on the six-person council that advised the viceroy. It also increased the number of Indians allowed to vote, and it gave Indian-controlled councils a greater say in local affairs. The Act divided Indian opposition to the Raj by guaranteeing influence not only to Hindus but to such religious minorities as Muslims, Sikhs, and Christians.

▲ Delegates from India's Congress Party visit the British Houses of Parliament during the 1920's.

▶ In 1918, Secretary of State of India Edwin Samuel Montagu (1879-1924) and Viceroy of India Frederic Thesiger, Lord Chelmsford (1868-1933), suggested that self-governing institutions gradually be introduced in India. Many Indian nationalists thought the reforms did not go far enough. British conservatives thought they went too far.

[We] believe profoundly that the time has now come when the *sheltered* [protected] existence which we have given India cannot be prolonged without damage to her national life; . . . that the *placid* [calm], pathetic contentment of the masses is not the soil on which such Indian nationhood will grow.

from the Montagu-Chelmsford Report on Indian Constitutional Reform, 1918

3

In European countries, condonation [forgiving an offense] of such grievous [terrible] wrongs [as India has suffered] would have resulted in bloody revolution by the people. . . . Half of India is too weak to offer violent resistance and the other half is unwilling to do so . . . . I have therefore ventured to suggest a remedy of non-cooperation, which enables those who wish, to dissociate [end an association with] themselves from the Government and which, if it is unattended by violence and undertaken in an ordered manner, must compel [force] it [the Raj] to retrace its steps and undo the wrongs committed.

Mohandas Gandhi, 1920

◀ Gandhi sets out his policy of peaceful noncooperation (*satyagraha*) in a 1920 letter to the viceroy, Lord Chelmsford (1868-1933). Gandhi and other Congress Party leaders had rejected the Government of India Act of 1919 but were afraid of a fresh outbreak of the sort of violence that had led to the Amritsar Massacre. Gandhi's answer was not to fight the British but to refuse to cooperate with them. Gandhi believed that if enough people did this, the Raj would collapse.

4

▶ Gandhi (seated at the speaker's left) attends a meeting of the Muslim League in 1924. At the time, he was president of the Congress Party and believed strongly that Indian independence should not come at the cost of *partition* (division into two countries—one Hindu, one Muslim). To this end, he willingly participated with Muslims and included Muslims in talks about the path to *swaraj* (self-rule).

NOW YOU KNOW

- The Government of India Act in 1919 gave greater political power to some Indians living in British-controlled provinces.
- The Act reserved certain rights for the country's minorities.
- The Congress Party rejected the act but was worried about stirring up more violence.

Mohandas Gandhi

FOR ITS FIRST 25 YEARS, THE CONGRESS PARTY did not attract widespread support outside India's educated upper classes. The man mainly responsible for giving the party popular appeal was Mohandas Gandhi. A trained lawyer, Gandhi lived in South Africa from 1893 to 1914, where he developed ideas and tactics to gain Indian independence. His idea of passive resistance, which he called *satyagraha*, was rooted in Hinduism. It involved fighting all injustice—whether personal, social, economic, or political—by peaceful means. Gandhi's soulful presence, sharp intelligence, and belief in the basic goodness of the traditional Indian way of life attracted fellow countrymen of every class, caste, and religion.

◀ Mohandas Gandhi as a young man. Like many educated young Indians of his day, he adopted the dress and many of the customs of the British. Only later, after a long period of thought, did he abandon Western culture in favor of Indian culture.

2

Formerly, men worked in the open air only as much as they liked. Now thousands of workmen meet together and for the sake of their own maintenance, they work in factories or mines. Their condition is worse than that of beasts. They are obliged to work . . . at most dangerous occupations, for the sake of millionaires. Formerly, men were made slaves under physical *compulsion* [force]. Now they are enslaved by temptation of money and of the luxuries that money can buy.

Mohandas Gandhi, 1909

◀ In his 1909 book *Hind Swaraj*, Gandhi objected to Western ideas about success and money, arguing that money enslaved people. He thought all people should live in small, self-sufficient communities, making their own clothes and growing their own food. Gandhi himself adopted the lifestyle of an Indian peasant.

3

It is undoubtedly true that non-violence is spreading like the scent of . . . roses throughout the length and breadth of this land, but the foetid [stinking] smell of violence is still powerful, and it would be unwise to ignore or underrate it. The cause will prosper by this retreat. The movement had unconsciously drifted from the right path. We have come back to our moorings [attachments], and we can again go straight ahead.

Mohandas Gandhi, 1922

▶ Gandhi wrote in a 1922 letter of the need to end his campaign of noncooperation and return to nonviolence, after a group of his supporters set fire to a police station, killing 23 Indian policemen. Although backed by millions of Indians, *satyagraha* (passive resistance) was misunderstood by some of Gandhi's more hot-headed supporters who believed it involved ending the Raj by any means.

NOW YOU KNOW

- By 1920, Mohandas Gandhi was India's most powerful Indian politician and leader of the anti-British movement.
- Gandhi's philosophy of *satyagraha* meant ending injustice by peaceful noncooperation.
- The first campaign of noncooperation, 1920-1922, ended when it triggered violence.

Divided Campaigners

INDIAN NATIONALISTS DID NOT SPEAK WITH ONE VOICE. Some nationalists saw Gandhi's dream of a peasant society as too *idealistic* (based upon fine ideas, but not practical). A more practical group in the Congress Party, led by Motilal Nehru (1861-1931) and Chittaranjan Das (1870-1925), founded the Swaraj Party in 1922, which supported a more forceful approach to gaining independence. On the other hand, many conservative Indians, especially the rulers of the princely states, were content for the British rule to continue. At first, India's Muslims feared independence, believing it would result in Muslims being overshadowed by the Hindu majority. However, by the 1930's, the Muslim League had adopted the "Two-Nation Theory," which called for the Raj to be divided into separate and independent countries—one Hindu, one Muslim.

1

For the Inspector-General to say that my mother "used insulting language to the Jailer and was impertinent [rude]" shows that he is strangely lacking in a sense of proportion [the proper relationship between things], knows little of Indian society, and is not happy in the use of language. On no account am I prepared to take the slightest risk of further insult to my mother and wife. Under the circumstances the only course open to me is not to have any interviews. . . . I shall be glad if the Officiating [acting] Inspector-General will take the trouble to spell my name correctly in the future.

Jawaharlal Nehru, 1922

◀ In a 1922 letter to the superintendent of Dehra Dun prison, Jawaharlal Nehru (1889-1964), a highly educated lawyer, shows his scorn for his British persecutors. Jawaharlal supported Gandhi's passive resistance campaign and served a total of nine years in prison for *civil disobedience* (deliberate and public refusal to obey a law). He did not break with the Congress Party when his father, Motilal, left in 1922 to co-found the Swaraj Party. As Congress Party president, Jawaharlal supported the civil disobedience tactic that would eventually bring about political reforms.

2

▶ Motilal Nehru poses with his wife, Swarup Rani, and their young son, Jawaharlal, in an 1899 photograph. Motilal came from a wealthy family and adopted British customs. Nevertheless, he and his son worked hard for Indian independence. Jawaharlal became India's first prime minister; his daughter, Indira Gandhi, and her son, Rajiv Gandhi, also served as prime minister.

3

Life loses half its interest if there is no struggle . . . . The uncertainties of life are not appalling [terrifying] to one who has not, at heart, worldly ambitions. Moreover, it is not possible to serve one's country in the best and fullest manner if one is chained to the Civil Service.

Subhas Chandra Bose, 1920

◀ Subhas Chandra Bose (1897-1945) wrote to his brother in a 1920 letter that he left his position in the Indian Civil Service because he did not want to support the Raj in any way. A leader in the Indian independence movement, Bose rejected the passive resistance tactics of Gandhi and the Nehrus. Bose demanded immediate independence. This radical position led him to support the Axis powers (Germany, Italy, and Japan) in World War II (1939-1945). He even raised an army of Indians to fight on the side of the Axis against Britain.

▶ Mohandas Gandhi (center) on his famous Salt March of 1930. The 240-mile (386-kilometer) walk was a protest against the British salt tax. It drew attention to the independence movement. Thousands of people joined the march to Dandi, where they made salt from salt water without paying a tax. The march triggered protests all over India, resulting in 80,000 people, including Gandhi, being arrested.

4

NOW YOU KNOW

- The Indian nationalist movement was divided into a number of strands, though Gandhi remained the leading figure.
- By the 1930's, India's Muslims were beginning to demand an independent state separate from Hindus.
- The Raj's most extreme opponents later made common cause with the regimes of Germany and Japan during World War II.

A New Constitution

B Y THE END OF THE 1920'S, THERE WAS A MOVEMENT within the Congress Party that called for India to be granted dominion within the British Commonwealth. Dominions were self-governing nations with close ties to Britain. In 1928, the Congress Party issued the Nehru Report, written by Motilal Nehru, demanding immediate dominion status. Both Britain and India's Muslims, who were ever fearful of a Hindu take-over, rejected this. Three conferences held in London produced little agreement. Finally in 1935, the British government responded with the Government of India Act, which divided India into 11 nearly self-governing, democratic provinces. Britain, however, kept control of defense and foreign affairs.

1

The Congress stands today for full democracy in India and fights for a democratic state, not for socialism [a system that emphasizes state ownership of property]. It is anti-imperialist [against the rule or authority of one country over other countries and colonies] and strives for great changes in our political and economic structure. . . . But the urgent and vital problem for us today is political independence and the establishment of a democratic state. And because of this, the Congress must line up with all the progressive forces of the world and must stand for world peace.

Jawaharlal Nehru, 1936

◀ In a Dec. 27, 1936, speech to the Congress Party, Jawaharlal Nehru states that India's first objective should be independence and democracy, not any specific political doctrine, such as socialism. However, he did not address the fears of such minorities as Muslims and Sikhs, who were afraid of losing their rights in a Congress-dominated Hindu democracy. In the last sentence, Nehru rejects forming alliances with *totalitarian governments* (governments that suppress all opposition), such as Germany and Japan.

2

▶ A political dynasty in the making: Jawaharlal Nehru, president of the Congress Party, with his daughter, Indira, in 1937. Soon after, Indira Nehru left to study at Oxford University in the United Kingdom. In time, both father and daughter would serve as prime minister of an independent India.

3

It is alarming and also nauseating [sickening] to see Mr. Gandhi, a seditious [stirring up rebellion] Middle Temple [one of the legal areas of London] lawyer, now posing as a fakir [a Hindu holy man] of a type well-known in the East, striding half-naked up the steps of the viceregal palace, while he is still organizing and conducting a defiant campaign of civil disobedience, to parley [talk] on equal terms with the representative of the King-Emperor.

Winston Churchill, 1931

◀ Winston Churchill, addressing the West Essex Conservative Association (an English political group) on Feb. 23, 1931, attempts to discredit Gandhi by describing him as a middle-class lawyer who pretended to be poor and of the common people. British conservatives like Winston Churchill were bitterly opposed to the 1935 Government of India Act, which granted India some degree of independence.

4

▶ After enjoying a promising early career as a government minister, Winston Churchill was by the 1930's widely considered an out-of-touch "has-been." During this period, he held two highly unpopular opinions: he fiercely opposed the rise of Nazism in Germany, and he strongly opposed independence for India. Time would prove him right about Nazism. However, his attitude about India and the British Empire remained firmly rooted in the ideas of the century into which he had been born—the 1800's. He was proved wrong on India.

NOW YOU KNOW

- Many members of the Congress Party believed that India should one day be a dominion.
- The Government of India Act (1935) introduced some measure of independence and democracy but kept key powers in British hands.
- Many conservatives in Britain opposed any measure of Indian independence.

The Idea of Pakistan

ISLAM AND HINDUISM DIFFERED IN BELIEFS ABOUT RELIGION and over such practical issues as family life and education. Although *confrontation* (direct fighting) between the two groups was checked by the British Raj, Muslims feared that independence would lead to a loss of rights—or even persecution. The leader of the Muslim League, Mohammad Ali Jinnah (1876-1948), tried several times to reach a compromise with the Congress Party. After the 1937 elections, he offered the Congress Party an alliance: Both bodies would work together for independence; but Congress had to share power and recognize the League as the sole representative of India's Muslims. When Congress Party leaders refused, Jinnah decided it was time to make a stand. This meant striving for a separate Muslim nation apart from India—Pakistan.

◄ Mohammad Ali Jinnah as a law student in London. Jinnah was the most *formidable* (not easily defeated) of India's Muslim leaders. He played a key role in negotiating the Lucknow Pact (1916) by which Hindus and Muslims agreed to work together to weaken British control over India. However, by 1937 he had changed his mind about cooperation with the Congress Party. In 1940, he backed the Muslim League's Lahore Resolution, which called for greater Muslim *autonomy* (self-government) within British India. Many historians have interpreted the resolution as a demand for a separate Muslim nation.

▶ Jinnah expresses the idea that Gandhi's term for self-rule—swaraj—suggests Hindu-Muslim unity. He notes, however, that Hindus and Muslims are not and never have been unified, which is how India fell under foreign rule in the first place. He says they will never be united because they do not trust each other. Jinnah was right: when India gained independence in 1947, violence between Muslims and Hindus left hundreds of thousands of people dead (see pages 36-41).

2

For the advent of foreign rule and its continuance in India, is primarily due to the fact that the people of India, particularly the Hindus and Mohamedans [Muslims], are not united and do not sufficiently trust each other. . . . Swaraj is [an] almost interchangeable term with Hindu-Muslim unity.
Mohammad Ali Jinnah, 1924

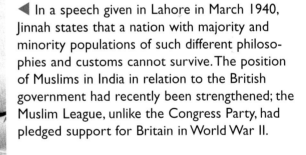

3

The Hindus and Muslims belong to two different religious philosophies, social customs and literature. They neither intermarry, nor dine together and, indeed, they belong to two different civilisations, which are based mainly on conflicting ideas. . . . To yoke [join] together two such nations under a single state, one as a minority and one as a majority, must lead to growing discontent and final destruction of . . . such a state.
Mohammad Ali Jinnah, 1940

◀ In a speech given in Lahore in March 1940, Jinnah states that a nation with majority and minority populations of such different philosophies and customs cannot survive. The position of Muslims in India in relation to the British government had recently been strengthened; the Muslim League, unlike the Congress Party, had pledged support for Britain in World War II.

NOW YOU KNOW

- Deep-rooted tensions existed between India's Muslim and Hindu communities for centuries.
- For years, Mohammad Ali Jinnah, the outstanding leader of the Muslim League, worked for a single independent Indian nation within which Muslim rights would be guaranteed.
- By 1940, the Muslim League was working for a separate and independent Muslim homeland.

World War II

GOING AGAINST THE SPIRIT OF THE 1935 GOVERNMENT OF INDIA ACT, the viceroy, Lord Linlithgow (1887-1952), declared in September 1939 that India was at war with Germany and Italy. Indians were shocked and faced a difficult decision. The vast majority of Indians did not support *fascism*, yet they objected to Britain making such crucial decisions for them. (Fascism is a system of government in which industry and labor are regulated and all opposition is suppressed.) Gandhi was opposed to the war based upon his views on nonviolence. The Congress Party agreed to support war if granted immediate independence. The Muslim League fully backed the war. Extreme nationalists, led by Chandra Bose, prepared to work with Britain's enemies to achieve independence.

1

It is quite clear that you are today the one person in the world who can prevent a war which may reduce humanity to the savage state. Must you pay that price for an object however worthy it may appear to you to be? Will you listen to the appeal of one who has deliberately shunned the method of war not without considerable success?

Mohandas Gandhi, 1939

◀ In a July 1939 letter to German leader Adolf Hitler, Mohandas Gandhi shows the depth of his feelings about nonviolence as he asks Hitler to prevent another war. Gandhi also urged Britain to negotiate with Hitler's Germany, convinced that all violence, even resistance to extreme *tyranny* (forms of government by rulers who have unrestricted power), was wrong. His views were ignored by Hitler and were given little weight in Britain, especially after Winston Churchill became prime minister in May 1940.

▶ A Congress Party Working Committee report shows how the party hoped to use the outbreak of war to force Britain to grant India full independence. In fact, the opposite took place. When the British government rejected the Congress Party's proposal, all party officials were ordered to resign from their posts and the Raj resumed direct rule over India for the first time since 1919.

2

A free democratic India will gladly associate herself with other free nations for mutual *defence* [the British spelling for defense] against aggression and for economic cooperation, but cooperation must be between equals and by mutual consent.

from a Congress Party Working Committee report, 1939

▲ Engineers from Bengal work with other Allied troops (visible in the background) to repair a road that has been blown up by the retreating enemy in Bardia, in Libya, 1942. During the independence negotiations that followed five years later, Bengalis hoped that their brave war effort would persuade the British to grant Bengal independence from the rest of India.

NOW YOU KNOW

- The United Kingdom declared war on India's behalf in September 1939.
- The British government rejected the Congress Party's offer of wartime support in return for Indian independence.
- With the Raj governing India directly, Bose's Forward Block Party was prepared to ally itself to Britain's totalitarian enemies—Germany and Japan.

Industry and Famine

ALTHOUGH ACCURATE EVIDENCE IS DIFFICULT TO COME BY and is controversial, many Indian nationalists felt that the British exploited India to help with their war effort. The Indian subcontinent provided a base for supplying the hard-pressed army of the Soviet Union, and manufactured goods and food from India were exported in large quantities to support the Allies. India did get some benefits. Electric-power output in the country doubled and the steel plant at Jamshedpur, in eastern India, became the Empire's leading producer. Yet, a terrible famine occurred in Bengal—a state in the eastern region of India that was eventually divided between the country of Bangladesh and the Indian state of West Bengal. That famine has also been blamed on the war. It killed between 1½ and 3 million people in 1943.

◀ Peasants remain close to starvation fully two years after the terrible famine that had led to so many deaths in Bengal in 1943. Whatever the true causes of the famine, the ruling British Raj was held responsible. Many Indians believed that with independence such suffering would never be repeated.

▶ Bengali author Manik Bandyopadhyay (1908-1956) describes the effects of the 1943 Bengal famine in a short story. Whether or not the British war effort was partly responsible for the Bengal famine, many Indians blamed the Raj for the disaster. Historians now say that it had complex causes: rice imports from Burma (now Myanmar) ended after that country was occupied by the Japanese in 1942; food was exported from India to feed troops; a cyclone destroyed crops; supplies were hoarded; and the local administration was incompetent.

Not one, not ten, but hundreds, hundreds of thousands, they went to their deaths. They stretched their hands to beg, tossed in the pain of hunger, they begged for the gruel drained off cooked rice to make it fluffy, they fought with stray dogs pawing through rotting dumps. . . .

Manik Bandyopadhyay, mid-1940's

3

Bengal famine was one of the greatest disasters that has befallen any people under British rule and damage to our reputation here . . . is incalculable [not measurable]. . . . Attempt by His Majesty's Government to prove on the basis of admittedly defective statistics that we can do without help . . . would be regarded here by all opinion British and Indian as utterly indefensible [unable to be defended].

Field Marshall Archibald Wavell, 1943

◀ A telegram from Lord Wavell (1883-1950), who became viceroy in 1943, to Winston Churchill's government in London makes it clear that the British were being blamed for the famine and begs for assistance. Churchill was extremely unhelpful, asking why, if food was so scarce, Gandhi had not yet died. Eventually Churchill *relented* (gave in), and the famine ended when 1 million tons (907,000 metric tons) of grain was shipped to Bengal.

▶ Indian students make shells for the British war effort in a government technical school. The photograph was originally published in *The Illustrated War News* under the title "The loyal devotion of India to the common heritage." Many Indians considered contributing to the war effort as a way to gain independence.

4

NOW YOU KNOW

- Indian industry and farming helped greatly in the Allied war effort.
- The Raj was held responsible for a famine that killed between 1½ and 3 million people.
- Winston Churchill's wartime government kept India and its welfare low on its list of priorities.

Quit India

BY EARLY 1942, JAPANESE ARMIES WERE SWEEPING THE FAR EAST. Churchill's government, desperate to secure India's full support, came under pressure from U.S. President Franklin D. Roosevelt to meet Congress Party's demands. Reluctantly, Churchill sent Sir Stafford Cripps (1889-1952) to India in March 1942 with a not entirely sincere offer of independence immediately after the war. The Congress Party rejected the plan, and Gandhi launched another *satyagraha* (a philosophy and practice of nonviolent resistance) named "Quit India." The British responded by arresting nearly all of the Congress Party leadership, including Gandhi. This triggered a wave of arrests and violence that claimed hundreds of lives. Most of the Congress leaders spent the rest of World War II in jail. During this period, the Muslim League remained firmly behind the Raj, giving its leader, Mohammad Jinnah, a political advantage after the war.

1

> His Majesty's Government . . . have decided to lay down in precise and clear terms the steps which they propose shall be taken for the earliest possible *realization* [result] of self-government in India. The object is the creation of a new Indian Union which shall constitute a Dominion, associated with the United Kingdom and the other Dominions by a common allegiance to the Crown, but equal to them in every respect. . . .
>
> from Sir Stafford Cripps's offer of independence, 1942

◄ The British government's 1942 offer of independence fell short of the wishes of the Congress Party in several respects. It did not grant independence immediately, and it proposed an opt-out for any province or princely state that did not wish to be part of the new nation. The clause was partly to protect the Muslim community, which remained loyal to Britain throughout the war. For members of the Congress Party, however, it meant the Indian nation would be fragmented even before it was formed.

2

► Sir Stafford Cripps (left) meets with Congress Party President Maulana Azad (1888-1958) and Jawaharlal Nehru (right) in New Delhi, in 1942. Azad, an Arab-born Muslim, sided with Nehru in rejecting Cripps's offer of Dominion status. As one of the most prominent Muslim leaders to support Hindu-Muslim unity, Azad rejected Jinnah's call for a separate Muslim homeland. Days after the "Quit India" protests began, Azad, Nehru, and other Congress Party leaders were imprisoned by the British.

▲ Police fire tear gas to disperse Indians participating in a "Quit India" campaign protest in Bombay (Mumbai) in 1942. British Prime Minister Churchill, hostile to Indian unrest while Britain was at war, supported strong action against protests. One of the ironies of the Indian independence movement was the violence often triggered by Gandhi's calls for peaceful demonstrations.

▶ In an Aug. 8, 1942, speech quoted in the *Times* of London, Congress Party President Maulana Azad rejects the Cripps proposal. He suggests declaring independence and then allying India with the emerging United Nations. On the same day, the Congress Party backed Gandhi's *satyagraha*. Through the subsequent wave of riots, nearly all Indian police and soldiers remained loyal to Britain. Nevertheless, reinforcements were rushed in from abroad, and within two months, the *satyagraha* had been put down.

> Let us not depend upon promises. Let us have a declaration of Indian independence forthwith, and we on our part shall immediately enter into a treaty of alliance with the United Nations for the sole purpose of fighting and winning this war.
>
> Maulana Azad, 1942

NOW YOU KNOW

- U.S. President Franklin D. Roosevelt put pressure on Britain to grant Indian independence.

- In 1942, a British mission, led by Sir Stafford Cripps, offered India independence after the war.

- The Congress Party rejected Cripps's proposal. A short-lived wave of violence followed Gandhi's "Quit India" *satyagraha* and the arrest of nearly the entire Congress Party leadership.

Deadlock

A<small>FTER</small> W<small>ORLD</small> W<small>AR</small> II, I<small>NDIAN INDEPENDENCE SEEMED INEVITABLE</small>. But talks held in June 1945 between Viceroy Wavell and Indian leaders collapsed over the usual difficult problem: How could the Muslim minority feel secure in a Hindu-dominated country? In 1945, the British Labour Party won control of the House of Commons, and Winston Churchill was out as prime minister. The new Labour prime minister, Clement Atlee (1883-1967), was reluctant to grant independence to India without a definite idea of what the new government would be like. In 1946, Atlee's government suggested an All-India Union with a limited central government and three types of provincial government.

◀ Gandhi visits political prisoners in Calcutta's Dum-Dum prison in December 1945. The tactic of imprisoning the leaders of the independence movement from time to time had little effect. It put a huge strain on police resources and drew attention to the prisoners' cause by turning them into victims of imperial power.

▶ At a meeting in Simla (now Shimla) in 1946, a delegation of Atlee's Cabinet members met with representatives from various Indian groups and suggested an All-India Union government, known as the Cabinet Mission Plan. The plan assigned powers not given to the Union to provincial governments in three clusters: the predominantly Hindu areas, such as Madras (now Chennai); the predominantly Muslim areas, such as Sind; and areas where people of differing religions were more equally mixed, such as Bengal and Assam. At first, Jawaharlal Nehru tried to sell the plan to his followers by suggesting that the guarantees to safeguard Muslims were doomed to failure.

There should be a Union of India, embracing both British India and the States [the Princely States], which should deal with the following subjects: foreign affairs, defence, and communications; and should have the powers necessary to raise the finances required for the above subjects.

statement by the Cabinet Mission and his Excellency the Viceroy, 1946

▶ The Muslim League rejected the Mission Plan after Nehru had rejected it. "It was fantastic," Nehru stated, "for the Mission to think they could tell Indians what to do ten years from now." Nehru was speaking of the British attempt to create a system of checks and balances to guarantee the safety of religious minorities, such as Muslims. The rejection of the Mission Plan by both groups proved to be a major step towards a divided India.

3

The attitude of Congress [the Congress Party] clearly shows that these conditions . . . for the successful working of the constitution-making body do not exist. This fact, taken together with the policy of the British Government of sacrificing the interests of the Muslim nation . . . leaves no doubt that . . . the participation of the Muslims in the proposed [constitution] is *fraught* [loaded] with danger and the Council, therefore, hereby withdraws its acceptance of [the British] Cabinet Mission's proposals.

statement by the Council of the Muslim League, 1946

4

◀ The empty seats in the 1946 meeting of India's Central Legislative Assembly were the result of a Muslim League boycott. The boycott, which was called after the Muslim League rejected the Mission Plan, was the start of a political movement called "Direct Action" to *partition* (divide) India and create an independent Pakistan.

NOW YOU KNOW

- After the war, most involved parties accepted that India should be independent. However, there was still no agreement on how to safeguard the rights of religious minorities.
- The proposed All-India Union or "Mission Plan" met some acceptance in mid-1946.
- After the Congress Party rejected the Plan's checks and balances to safeguard Muslim rights, the Muslim League rejected the All-India Union and began a political movement for an independent Pakistan.

Direct Action

BY REJECTING THE ALL-INDIA UNION, OR MISSION PLAN, the Muslim League was, in reality, insisting on a separate Muslim country, as opposed to a state within the larger nation of India. To demonstrate Muslim unity behind this demand, Jinnah called on the "Muslim nation" to make Aug. 16, 1946, a "day of direct action" of marches and protests. The demonstrations remained peaceful in most parts of India, but in Calcutta (now Kolkata) they turned into a bloodbath. Muslim gangs turned on Hindus, who in turn slaughtered Muslims. From Calcutta, the violence spread across India, and civil war *loomed* (appeared large and dangerous). Although Viceroy Wavell came close to persuading Nehru and Jinnah to join an interim government, the British government lost faith in Wavell and he was relieved of his post.

▶ In Jinnah's July 1946 call for "direct action," he states that all constitutional methods, and all appeals to tribunals have failed. The only tribunal left is the Muslim nation of India. Jinnah had no intention that his call for marches and protests would turn violent, but the movement launched India into its worst civil unrest since 1857.

1

Never have we in the whole history of the League done anything except by constitutional methods and by constitutionalism. But now . . . we bid goodbye to constitutional methods. We have exhausted all reason. There is no tribunal [court of justice appointed to examine special evidence] to which we can go. The only tribunal is the Muslim Nation.

Mohammad Ali Jinnah, 1946

2

More than 1,000 persons have been killed and more than 4,000 injured in the Calcutta riots which began during the Muslim *hartal* [protest] on Friday.

These figures were given by a high police officer in Calcutta yesterday, when fresh disorders broke out and Hindus began to hit back at the Muslims.

The Times, Aug. 19, 1946

◀ The figures given an Aug. 19, 1946, published in the London newspaper *The Times*, proved wildly inaccurate. During the three days following Jinnah's Direct Action Day, between 4,000 and 7,000 people were killed in Calcutta alone. Around 100,000 others were injured. Racial killings also erupted in Bombay and Karachi the following month.

▲ Calcutta policemen use tear gas to put down the riots in the city in August 1946. The violence broke out after Hindu and Muslim leaders disagreed over the terms of Indian independence, and the leader of the Muslim League called for "direct action." In days of rioting, local gangs of both religions used the prospect of *partition* (dividing India into two countries) to settle old scores.

NOW YOU KNOW

- Seeking a show of Muslim unity, Jinnah called for Aug. 16, 1946, to be a day of direct action for Muslims.
- In Calcutta, the Muslim demonstrations quickly turned into full-scale riots in which thousands died.
- Viceroy Wavell was removed from his post early in 1947.

Partition

IN MARCH 1947, LORD LOUIS MOUNTBATTEN (1900-1979) was named India's last viceroy. A naval officer and great-grandson of Queen Victoria, Mountbatten had personal charm and self-confidence. He was close to the British royal family and had engineered the marriage of his nephew, Prince Philip (1921-   ), to Princess Elizabeth (1926-   ), heir to the throne. After becoming viceroy, Mountbatten found a friend in Nehru but grew to dislike Jinnah. Mountbatten soon decided partition was inevitable and that to avoid civil war the 1948 target date for independence had to be moved forward. In July 1947, the British Parliament duly passed the Indian Independence Act, transferring power at midnight on August 14-15, 1947. Boundary commissions had just one month to divide the Raj into two countries, Pakistan and India.

◀ Lord Louis Mountbatten reviews the governor general's bodyguard at Viceroy House in New Delhi, as he takes up his position as viceroy of India.

▶ In a letter to Mountbatten, Wavell's remarks about getting women and children out first and the army last reveal he understood that violence was inevitable. Mountbatten's first plan followed Wavell's idea: British forces would withdraw, leaving each state to decide its future for itself. Nehru rejected the idea as a recipe for chaos.

I have tried everything I know to solve the problem of handing over India to its people; and I can see no light. I have only one solution, which I call Operation Madhouse—withdrawal of the British province by province, beginning with women and children, then civilians, then the army.

Viceroy Wavell, 1947

▶ Nehru's remarks in a May 1947 letter to Mountbatten show his unhappiness with the idea of a partitioned India. He predicted, rightly, that it would lead to conflict. The speed with which the India-Pakistan border was drawn made matters worse. The border was drawn by Hindu and Muslim judges headed by an Englishman. The boundaries they produced attempted to place most Hindus in India and most Muslims in Pakistan. As they had unreliable information about populations, the lines they drew were inaccurate. Many of India's 6 million Sikhs also wanted their own homeland, which the partition failed to produce.

The whole approach was completely different . . . and the picture of India that emerged frightened me. In fact much that we had done so far was undermined . . . and an entirely new picture presented—a picture of fragmentation [the process of breaking into fragments] and conflict and disorder, and unhappily also, of a worsening of relations between India and Britain.

Jawaharlal Nehru, 1947

◀ Press representatives view the Katra Jaimal Singh, a wholesale market, in ruins following the violence on Amritsar in March 19, 1947. The unrest leading up to and during partition was particularly acute in the Punjab, where rioting broke out between Sikhs, Hindus, and Muslims. Much damage was done in Amritsar, the Punjab city of the Golden Temple of the Sikhs, making it necessary for the military to take control.

NOW YOU KNOW

- Mountbatten, appointed last viceroy of India in 1947, decided the country had to be partitioned at the time of independence.

- In a hurry to get out, Britain passed the Indian Independence Act in July 1947.

- Boundary commissions set the borders between India and Pakistan just weeks before independence at midnight on Aug. 14-15, 1947.

Yet More Violence

AS SOON AS THE DECISION TO DIVIDE INDIA WAS MADE, violence exploded. In many regions, especially Bengal in the east of India and the Punjab in the northwest, gangs attacked people of other faiths simply to steal their goods, houses, and land. The police and military were overwhelmed. Moreover, with the days of the Raj ending, loyalty to community began replacing loyalty to the British Crown. This community loyalty meant that soldiers often refused to act against mobs of the same religion as themselves. The number of victims will never be known, but the evidence suggests that between 500,000 and 1 million people were killed during the violent time of partition.

1

My daughters were clinging to me and holding my sari tight. The Moslems threw us outside. They carried away my three eldest daughters. The eldest was beaten on the head. She stretched her hands to me and cried: "Ma, Ma." I could not move. Some time later the Moslems took my husband and son from the train and threw them into the well.

wife of a Hindu schoolmaster

◀ In her recollections of March 1947, the wife of a Hindu schoolmaster describes mob violence aboard a train. When her family heard that their home state, Punjab, had been placed within the Muslim nation of Pakistan, they tried to leave by train. Only 100 of the 2,000 passengers on their train made it to India alive.

2

▶ One detail of a Hindu man's recollection about Calcutta at the time of the partition reveals how "normal" violence had become during this period: The worshipers in the Ganges River simply ignore that two men are being murdered next to them and continue with their prayers.

Followed by a crowd waving clubs, knives and iron bars, the two wretched [Muslim] men were herded down the street. . . . "In normal times," their 17-year-old captor later declared, "we would not have polluted the sacred water [of the Ganges River] with Moslem blood". . . . They pushed the victims into the water. . . . One man fought for his life. "The same boy hit him on the head," the chief assassin recalled. "Children threw bricks in his face. Another stabbed him in the neck to be very sure he was dead." Around the site the Hindu worshippers continued their prayers.

a Hindu man's recollection of Hindu on Muslim violence, 1947

▲ Working parties clear the bodies of victims of violence from the streets of Delhi in September 1947. The arrival of independence brought joy and sorrow in equal measure as the beatings, rapes, murders, and robberies continued long after the British had lowered their flag over India's capital, New Delhi.

NOW YOU KNOW

- The decision to partition India along religious lines led to terrible violence.
- In some places, the law completely broke down because soldiers often refused to act against mobs of the same religion as themselves.
- Although there are no reliable figures, it is thought that between 500,000 and 1 million people died in India's worst violence in modern times.

Refugees

A T FIRST, NO ONE KNEW WHERE THE MUSLIM HOMELAND of Pakistan would be or whether it would be an entirely new country or an independent part of India. In the end, it became a separate country in two parts. West Pakistan was fashioned from Sind (in the northwest), part of Punjab (in the northwest), and neighboring territory. East Pakistan was created largely from eastern Bengal (in eastern India). Many boundaries were uncertain. For the princely states the choice of whether to join India or Pakistan depended on the decision of the ruling prince. In the chaos, some 15 million desperate people left home in an effort to get somewhere they would feel safe. Many relocated to a place with which they had little cultural connection.

▲ Refugees wildly overcrowd trains in an attempt to reach safety on the other side of the religious border in the fall of 1947. For many, the journey would be their last. On September 21, Muslims attacked a refugee train at Harbanspura and killed 1,500 non-Muslims; the next day, Sikhs attacked a "bulging, writhing" trainload of Muslim refugees at Amritsar, killing hundreds; two days later, Muslims carried out a revenge attack on a Sikh and Hindu train, killing hundreds more.

2

We came across to India from Dhaka in 1947. Our house was burnt down and my parents' lands were seized. I was a newlywed. I wore my wedding sari on the freighter we took across the Bay of Bengal. There were thousands of people on the boat, people were falling off into the water and drowning as we crossed to India at night. Along the coast we could see houses being burnt. As we fled Dhaka, I remember dead bodies being burnt by the roadside. I remember the screams of a Hindu family, our neighbours, being burnt alive in their home.

The Observer, 2007

◀ Speaking to the British newspaper *The Observer*, the Indian woman Visaka Das recalls becoming a refugee in 1947 upon leaving her home city of Dhaka after it had been made part of East Pakistan. An estimated 7 million Muslim refugees flooded into Pakistan in 1947, while roughly the same number of non-Muslims, such as Visaka Das, fled in the opposite direction. For many of the refugees, rebuilding a new life in a new land would prove difficult. When Visaka Das was interviewed in 2007, she was still living in the refugee camp she had moved into after fleeing Pakistan 60 years earlier.

▶ In a first-person account later published in a book, artist and writer Amarnath Sehgal (1922-2007) describes fleeing the western Punjab city of Lahore for eastern Punjab. Along the way, he was horrified to find that thousands of Muslim refugees wishing to go west (from India to Pakistan) were killed before they could escape. The Boundary Commission had haphazardly split Punjab between Pakistan and India. As a result, some 10 million Punjabis—Hindus, Sikhs, and Muslims—ended up refugees.

3

When I arrived in eastern Punjab things were no better [than in Lahore]. In the Kangra-Kulu Valley a wholesale slaughter of the Muslim minority took place between August and September [1947]. Out of 35,000 only 9,000 [Muslims] managed to escape alive to Pakistan. The River Beas was littered with dead bodies and a foul odour was in the air for weeks after the massacres.

Amarnath Sehgal, 1947

NOW YOU KNOW

- Drafting Pakistan's borders was not well planned.
- In a few confusing months, millions of people moved across the new borders in an effort to find somewhere safe to live.
- The mass migration of people resulted in loss of goods and property, terrible suffering, and massive numbers of deaths.

Princely Decisions

MUCH OF INDIA HAD BEEN ONLY INDIRECTLY RULED BY THE BRITISH. There were also hundreds of semi-independent princely states, all loyal to the Raj and hostile to the idea of being swallowed up within India or Pakistan. The British secretary of state for India, Lord Listowel (1906-1997), agreed that the princes could become fully independent. Lord Mountbatten overruled him and told the princes that they had a simple choice: join either India or Pakistan. In return they would receive privileges and huge payments. The majority of the princes accepted that offer. There were some states that did not immediately join either country. The last princely state to give up its independence, Sikkim, did not join India until 1975.

▲ A prince of Rajputana (now Rajasthan) in western India rides in his wedding procession just months after independence. Although such princes lost most of their political power, their wealth and influence remained largely intact. Their lavish lifestyles and opulent displays of wealth raised difficult questions in a country where the great majority of people lived near or in extreme poverty.

2

I too will be grieved if I find that Your Highness refuses to accede [accept] before 14 August, since I shall bitterly feel the fatal isolation of an old friend; and it would be sad that you or your illustrious [outstanding] family would travel without any diplomatic privileges unless Your Highness were able to set up legations or consulates [diplomatic offices] in various parts of the world.

Lord Louis Mountbatten, c. 1947

◀ In a letter to the Maharaj Rana of Dholpur (in east-central India), Lord Louis Mountbatten subtly threatens to strip the prince of certain diplomatic privileges unless the prince caves in to the viceroy's demand that Dholpur join India. The letter is typical of the way Mountbatten flattered and threatened the princes into joining one of the new countries. During this period, a civil service official ordered the burning of tons of government documents in which the British had kept records of the various indiscretions and wrongdoings of the rulers of the princely states. The British government did not want the Congress Party to use the information to blackmail the princes after independence.

3

Dickie's [Lord Mountbatten's] form simply came in the post one day and I signed it and sent it back. What else could we have done? We had no access to the sea and could never have operated alone; it was a case of accept the change or die.

the Nawab of Palanpur

▶ With these words, Taley Mohammed Khan (1882-1957), nawab (a princely title) of Palanpur, explains why he signed the paper that made his princely state part of India. He had no choice: landlocked Palanpur could not exist alone.

NOW YOU KNOW

- The leaders of India's hundreds of princely states, loyal to the Raj, were not happy surrendering their political power.

- Mountbatten used various methods to pressure the princes to join India or Pakistan immediately.

- The princes were also bribed with wealth and privileges to surrender their political power.

Punjab and Bengal

IN TWO REGIONS, PUNJAB AND BENGAL, PARTITION CAUSED SPECIAL DIFFICULTIES. In the west, the rich and fertile Punjab consisted of 40 separate princely states within the Punjab States Agency, a British administration unit. Punjab was home to some 28 million Muslims, 10 million Hindus, and 5 million Sikhs. A Sikh political party—the Akali Dal—tried unsuccessfully to carve out in western Punjab a homeland for people of that religion, but the area was given to Pakistan. On the Indian-West Pakistani border, some 7.5 million Hindus and Sikhs entered India, and some 7 million crossed the other way. In the east, some 65 million people lived in the huge and densely populated Bengal region. At partition, it was divided with much bloodshed. West Bengal remained in India, and East Bengal formed the bulk of East Pakistan.

1

The Sikhs form a compact cultural nationality of about six millions. They further maintain that . . . the Punjab is not only their homeland, but their holy land. They were the last rulers of the Punjab and . . . they enjoyed in the Punjab independent economic and political status which has gradually deteriorated [come apart] under British rule . . . [Therefore] the statutory [a thing fixed by law, or statute] Muslim majority in the legislature of the Province must go and the position of the Sikhs must be strengthened. . . .
Master Tara Singh, 1946

◀ In a 1946 memorandum, the leader of the Akali Dal Party, Master Tara Singh (1885-1967), writes that the Punjab is both homeland and holy land of the Sikhs. He argues that to hold it, Sikhs must strengthen their position in relation to the Muslim majority in the legislature. Singh's party lost much sympathy in 1947 when its members began slaughtering and driving out thousands of Muslims to gain a purely Sikh territory. In the end, Muslims retaliated by killing huge numbers of Sikhs and forcing the rest to flee to East Punjab as penniless refugees.

▶ Mohammad Ali Jinnah, leader of the Muslim League, warns Lord Mountbatten that to split the Punjab and Bengal will lead to endless trouble. Most likely, he wanted all of both states incorporated into Pakistan. The eventual solution—splitting the Punjab and creating East Pakistan out of East Bengal—pleased few people. After a short war of independence, East Bengal broke away from Pakistan to form Bangladesh in 1971.

2

Your Excellency [referring to Lord Mountbatten] doesn't understand. A man is a Punjabi or a Bengali before he is a Hindu or Moslem. They share a common history, language, culture and economy. You must not divide them. You will cause endless bloodshed and trouble.
Mohammad Ali Jinnah, 1947

▲ Master Tara Singh, the leader of the Akali Dal movement, speaks at a conference in 1943. Singh sought a Sikh homeland in the Punjab before the partition. Although he failed to achieve that goal, he did live long enough to see Prime Minister Indira Gandhi (Nehru's daughter) in 1966 reorganize the boundaries of the Punjab state so that it contained a clear Sikh majority and included the Sikhs' holy city of Amritsar.

NOW YOU KNOW

- The Punjab and Bengal regions, with different religious groups living together, presented a problem for the independence settlement.
- Both states were divided between India and Pakistan, triggering terrible violence.
- The division of Punjab and Bengal between India and Pakistan pleased almost no one, and East Pakistan broke away from West Pakistan in 1971 to form Bangladesh.

Two Nations

THE BRITISH RAJ GRANTED BOTH INDIA AND PAKISTAN INDEPENDENCE at midnight on Aug. 14, 1947. Pakistan announced its independence a little before midnight and celebrates its independence on the 14th of August. India celebrates its independence on the 15th. With a population of approximately 330 million, India was by far the larger nation. Pakistan, divided in two parts separated by nearly 1,000 miles (1,600 kilometers) of a foreign land, had a population of around 70 million. This population grew by hundreds of thousands each week as Muslim refugees flooded into Pakistan from India. At the time, neither country had an official state religion nor a constitution. Independence having come about so quickly, much of the work necessary for creating a nation had barely begun.

▲ On Aug. 15, 1947, Lord Mountbatten swears in Jawaharlal Nehru as the first prime minister of an independent India. Lady Mountbatten stands behind her husband on the platform. The handover took place in the throne room at Viceroy's House (now Rashtrapati Bhavan or president's house), the viceregal palace in New Delhi, capital of the Raj.

▶ The Aug. 15, 1947, edition of the London newspaper *The Times* announces Indian and Pakistani independence. The writer was mistaken to refer to Pakistan as an "Islamic" state. Jinnah, sometimes called the founder of Pakistan, planned a secular nation, that is, one in which people of all faiths would be treated equally. He had demanded a separate state for Muslims because he feared Hindus would dominate an independent India.

India and Pakistan officially make their début on the world stage today. One is larger in population than Russia; the other is the largest Islamic state in the world. The creation of these two new States marks the close of one chapter and the opening of another in the long history of relations between India and Britain, yet this day has come in a way that has been a disappointment to many Indians. . . . The vision which they have always had of a strong, united India has proved impossible. . . .

The Times, Aug. 15, 1947

▶ Joyful crowds celebrate India's new-found independence in Calcutta on Aug. 21, 1947. However, links to the British government were in place another three years before India became a full republic. At that point, the position of governor general (the British ruler who had been viceroy prior to independence) ended and was replaced by a president. But, in India, the prime minister, not the president, holds the real power.

For many simple Indians the magic word independence meant a new world was at hand. Ranjit Lal, a peasant from Chatharpur, assured his children that "there will be much to eat now because India is free." People refused to pay bus fares, assuming they should now be free. A humble beggar walked into an enclosure reserved for foreign diplomats. A policeman asked him for his invitation. "Invitation?" he answered, "Why do I need an invitation? I have my independence. That's enough."

from *Freedom at Midnight: The Epic Drama of India's Struggle for Independence*

◀ Larry Collins and Dominique Lapierre write in *Freedom at Midnight: The Epic Drama of India's Struggle for Independence* that many Indians had a mistaken idea of what independence meant. At first, little changed. Many Britons remained in India, working as before. The great majority of Indian people remained miserably poor. It would be 50 years before India grew into a world economic power.

NOW YOU KNOW

- Independence came about very quickly.
- Pakistan and an independent India officially came into being at midnight on Aug. 14, 1947.
- Pakistan was a homeland for Muslims but was not officially an Islamic state.

Governor General Jinnah

MOHAMMAD ALI JINNAH, THE "FATHER OF PAKISTAN," was the key player in Pakistan's independence movement. For most of his political life, he worked with the Muslim League to achieve an independent India in which Hindus and Muslims could live together as equals. In 1946, he lost faith in the Congress Party's leaders, believing their aim was a "Hindu Raj"—an Indian government that would create policies that favored Hindus. Jinnah then devoted himself to establishing Pakistan as a free, democratic, and liberal homeland in which Muslims, and people of other faiths, would be able to live in peace and security.

◀ Very thin and ill, Mohammad Ali Jinnah is sworn in as the first governor general of Pakistan on Aug. 14, 1947. Although his role as governor general was officially ceremonial, he remained heavily involved in day-to-day matters, leading the government and negotiating with India to secure a swift end to the refugee problem.

If we want to make this great State of Pakistan happy and prosperous we should wholly and solely concentrate on the well-being of the people. . . . I think we should keep that in front of us as our ideal and you will find that in course of time Hindus would cease to be Hindus and Muslims would cease to be Muslims, not in the religious sense, because that is the personal faith of each individual, but in the political sense as citizens of the State.

Mohammad Jinnah, 1947

▶ Speaking to Pakistan's first Constituent Assembly (parliament) on Aug. 11, 1947, Mohammad Jinnah observes that personal faith is not a matter for the state. Already dying, he enjoyed the position of Pakistan's first governor general for little more than a year—not long enough to see his *secular* (not based in religion) ideas take firm root in Pakistan.

3

4

On the Indian side it was significant that when Mr Gandhi at his Tuesday prayer meeting tried to read some verses from the Koran he was shouted down by Sikh refugees and had to abandon the meeting. The *mahatma's* ["great Soul"] voice, it is worth noting, is the only one in India these days which is raised consistently and strongly against communal violence in all its forms.

The Times, Sept. 19, 1947

▲ The birth of a nation: Huge crowds throng the streets leading to the Constituent Assembly in Karachi as the country's first government is sworn in on Aug. 15, 1947. Karachi remained Pakistan's capital until Islamabad officially was named the capital in 1960.

◀ The Sept. 19, 1947, London newspaper *The Times* reports that Gandhi was shouted down when he tried to show his appreciation of Islam by reading from the Qur'ān in public. Like Jinnah, Gandhi dreamed of a united state shared equally by all faiths. Both leaders failed to fulfill their visions.

NOW YOU KNOW

- Mohammad Jinnah is regarded as the "Father of Pakistan."
- Jinnah believed in toleration between people of different religions.
- Jinnah was Pakistan's first governor general but died after a little over a year in office.

Kashmir

JAMMU AND KASHMIR (USUALLY SHORTENED TO KASHMIR) IN 1947 was a princely state in the Himalayan and the Karakoram mountains that included the fertile Kashmir Valley. Although the majority of the population was Muslim, the state also had many citizens of other faiths. The ruler, Maharaja Hari Singh (1895-1961), was Hindu. When faced with choosing between India and Pakistan, Singh hesitated in the hope of remaining independent. However, when his state was invaded by Pakistani armed forces and Pashtun tribal warriors in October 1947, Singh asked India for help. India refused its support unless Hari Singh joined India. He signed the Instrument of Accession on Oct. 26, 1947, making Kashmir part of India.

▶ Karan Singh (1931-), the son of Maharaja Hari Singh of Kashmir, describes his father finding ways to avoid meeting with Lord Mountbatten before independence. The maharaja's eventual *accession* (joining) to India remains controversial. Many Pakistanis believe Singh may never have signed the papers. Even if he did, they say, it was under pressure from India, whose troops already occupied his territory. Many Indians deny this, claiming Indian forces entered Kashmir only after Hari Singh signed the Instrument of Accession.

1

I suspect that in his heart my father still did not believe that the British would actually leave. . . . Instead of taking advantage of Mountbatten's visit to discuss the whole situation meaningfully, . . . he first sent the Viceroy out on a prolonged fishing trip . . . and then—having fixed a meeting just before his [Mountbatten's] departure—got out of it on the plea that he [the maharaja] had suddenly developed a severe attack of colic [severe stomach pain].

Karan Singh

2

Having heard statements on the situation in Kashmir from representatives of the Governments of India and Pakistan . . . in which they *affirmed* [stated] their intention to *conform* [act according to law or rule] to the Charter of the United Nations, [the Security Council] –

1. Calls upon both the Government of India and the Government of Pakistan to take immediately all measures within their power (including public appeals to their people) *calculated* [intended] to improve the situation.

United Nations Resolution 38, Jan. 17, 1948

◀ One of the first tasks of the newly formed United Nations was to broker peace between India and Pakistan over Kashmir. Resolutions 38 and 39 from January 1948 asked for a cease-fire and an agreement that the fate of the province be decided by a vote of its people. Because Pakistan still administered western Kashmir, India refused to cooperate in a vote. Since that time, Kashmiri history has become increasingly complicated, with periodic fighting for control between India and Pakistan. In 1962, Chinese troops seized part of eastern Kashmir.

▼ Pashtun warriors, from Pakistan's largely tribal North-West Frontier Province, operate with Pakistan commandos in the 1947 invasion of Kashmir. Pashtuns are an eastern Iranian ethnic group who live primarily in Afghanistan and Pakistan's frontier border areas. Many Muslims believed Kashmir should automatically have become part of Pakistan because 77 percent of its citizens were Muslim.

NOW YOU KNOW

- In 1947, the ruler of Kashmir was a Hindu, but the majority of his people were Muslim.
- Maharaja Hari Singh joined Kashmir with India after Pakistan invaded Kashmir.
- The India-Pakistan War of 1947-1948 over Kashmir settled nothing, and the territory has been disputed ever since.

Gandhi Assassinated

MOHANDAS GANDHI WAS BY FAR THE BEST KNOWN OF SOME HALF MILLION VICTIMS who died in the violence accompanying the collapse of the Raj. A Hindu *fanatic* (a person carried away beyond reason by his feelings or beliefs) assassinated Gandhi on Jan. 30, 1948, because the assassin hated the 78-year old Mahatma (great soul) for his tolerance toward Muslims. The most celebrated person in the independence story, Gandhi's stature as one of the foremost spiritual, political, moral, and cultural leaders of the 1900's is widely recognized throughout the world. His unique method of social change through nonviolent resistance has inspired countless others in their quest for justice and freedom.

1

Mr. Gandhi was walking from Birla House [in New Dehli] to the lawn at the back, where his evening prayer-meetings are held. . . . As he approached the waiting crowd a young man dressed in a khaki bush jacket and blue trousers greeted him from a distance of 5 ft [1.5 meters] with the customary Hindi salutation. . . . Gandhi smiled at him and according to one version, spoke to him. The young man then whipped out a pistol from an inside pocket and fired thrice at point blank range.

The Times, Jan. 31, 1948

◀ The Jan. 31, 1948, edition of the London newspaper *The Times* describes the details of Gandhi's assassination on January 30. The killer, Nathuram Godse (1910-1949), had links with extremist Hindu groups. He and a co-conspirator were found guilty of the murder and executed in November 1949. Gandhi's two sons had asked that their sentences be commuted because their execution would dishonor Gandhi's memory as a man of peace.

2

▶ Mahatma Gandhi meets with members of the Muslim League at Jahanabad, Bihar, in March 1947. His belief in religious toleration would cost him his life.

▶ In a radio speech by Jawaharlal Nehru after Gandhi's death on Jan. 30, 1948, India's prime minister describes him as the "father of the nation." Gandhi had succeeded in freeing India, but many of his hopes did not come to pass: Independence had come with terrible violence; and the Raj had been divided into two countries that would turn into bitter enemies.

The light has gone out of our lives and there is darkness everywhere. . . . Our beloved leader, Bapu [the Hindi word for "father"], as we called him, the Father of the Nation, is no more.

Jawaharlal Nehru, Jan. 30, 1948

◀ The flag of India, which Gandhi helped design, drapes his casket at his funeral. When Gandhi's son Ramdas set fire to the funeral pyre, and the logs burst into flames, the vast crowd groaned. Women wailed and men wept as his body was reduced to ashes. His death stopped the violence unleashed by independence, for a time. At the time of the assassination, physicist Albert Einstein wrote, "Generations to come will scarce believe that such a one as this ever in flesh and blood walked upon this earth."

NOW YOU KNOW

- Mohandas Gandhi was assassinated by a Hindu fanatic on Jan. 30, 1948.
- Gandhi's ideals have been a source of inspiration for millions.
- His doctrine of nonviolent resistance has been used repeatedly to effect social and political change.

India Since Independence

INDIA'S NEW CONSTITUTION WENT INTO EFFECT IN JANUARY 1950, when the Republic cut all links with the British government. In the more than half century since, Indian democracy has held firm, and a strong sense of national unity has developed. Although officially a *socialist nation* (a government system featuring public or community ownership of property), India avoided taking sides during the *Cold War* (a period of intense rivalry between Communist and non-Communist governments in the post-World War II era). Instead, it concentrated on industrialization. In recent years, India's rapidly growing economic power has made it a major player on the world stage.

1

And so we have to labour [the British spelling of labor] and to work, and work hard, to give reality to our dreams. Those dreams are for India, but they are also for the world, for all the nations and peoples are too closely knit together today for any one of them to imagine that it can live apart. Peace has been said to be indivisible; so is freedom, so is prosperity. . . .

Jawaharlal Nehru, 1947

◀ Speaking on the eve of independence, Aug. 14, 1947, Nehru suggests that Indian independence is significant for all nations. The independence of India marked not only the end of Western *imperialism* (a policy or action by which one country controls another country or territory), but also the beginning of an era of international cooperation. Sadly, Nehru's prophecy proved untrue as East and West moved into the Cold War. India, however, remained true to Nehru and took a position of non-alignment—siding with neither the capitalist West nor the Communist East.

▶ Indira Gandhi (1917-1984) was the daughter of Jawaharlal Nehru. (Her husband, politician Feroze Gandhi, was not related to Mohandas Gandhi.) She served as her father's unofficial chief of staff through much of his premiership. The year of his death, 1964, she was elected to parliament, and she became prime minister in 1966. She held office until 1977 and again from 1980 until her death. On Oct. 31, 1984, she was assassinated by two of her security guards, who were members of a Sikh separatist group. She was succeeded as premier by her son Rajiv (1944-1991). He too was assassinated, by a suicide bomber who was a *Tamil* separatist. (Tamils are an ethnic group of southern India and Sri Lanka.) Despite the turmoil, democracy held in India.

2

▶ In the Aug. 16, 2000, edition of the Indian newspaper, the *Deccan Herald*, journalist Kuldip Nayar (1924-) criticizes India's lack of economic progress in the last quarter century. While the middle class expanded, the bulk of the population of India remained very poor. Nayar's last sentence warns that this gulf between the rich and the poor threatens the unity of the nation and India's status as the world's largest democracy.

▼ Indian actress Madhuri Dixit (1967-) starred in *Devdas* (2002), the most expensive Bollywood film made up to that time. "Bollywood" (a combination of "*Bombay*" and "*Hollywood*") refers to the Hindu-language movie industry based in Mumbai (Bombay). Indian cuisine and Bollywood films, backed by the country's growing economic and industrial strength, have helped spread Indian culture around the world.

3

India has at present a larger population of poor than it had when it won freedom. The middle class has expanded but the economic benefits have not. In fact, the yawning gap between the haves and the have-nots has widened further. Even among the states, there is a growing *hiatus* [gap] which is telling upon the feeling of equality and unity in the country.

Kuldip Nayar, 2000

4

NOW YOU KNOW

- India cut all ties with the United Kingdom and adopted its constitution in January 1950.

- The Nehru-Gandhi family dominated Indian politics for nearly a half century.

- An independent India has grown in wealth and economic importance, but the gap between the rich and poor remains very wide.

Independent Pakistan

NEHRU'S PREDICTION THAT AN INDEPENDENT PAKISTAN could not survive proved unfounded. Nevertheless, the country has proved unstable, and democracy has never taken root there to the same extent as in India. Since independence, the country changed from a secular to an Islamic state. It has gone through alternating periods of democracy and dictatorship as power has seesawed back and forth between civilian governments and military rule. Endless border conflicts with India triggered an arms race that made both countries nuclear powers. In recent years, Pakistan has been destabilized by Islamic militants operating along its mountainous frontier with Afghanistan.

▶ The preamble to Pakistan's 1956 constitution declares that the state was founded on Islamic principles and that these principles included democracy and toleration. Nevertheless, the first military takeover in Pakistan took place in 1958 when General Mohammad Ayub Khan (1907-1974) seized power. He stayed in power until 1969. He was followed by another general, Yahya Khan, who held power until 1971. Since then, the country has experienced two additional periods of military rule (1977-1988 and 1999-2008) and three periods of elected government (1971-1977; 1988-1999; and from 2008).

In the name of *Allah* [God], the Beneficent [kindly], the Merciful

Whereas sovereignty over the entire Universe belongs to Allah Almighty alone. . . . Whereas the Founder of Pakistan, *Quaid-i-Azam* [Great Leader] Mohammad Ali Jinnah, declared that Pakistan would be a democratic State based on Islamic principles of social justice. . . . Wherein the Muslims of Pakistan should be enabled individually and *collectively* [together] to order their lives in accordance with the teachings and requirements of Islam. . . .

Wherein adequate provision should be made for the minorities freely to profess and practice their religion and develop their culture . . .

from the preamble to Pakistan's Constitution

◀ Awami League members raise a flag of independence on the balcony of their headquarters in Dacca (now Dhaka) in April 1971. The Awami League, a political party demanding independence, had won nearly every parliament seat allotted to East Pakistan in 1970. When West Pakistan leaders maneuvred to keep them out of the assembly, war broke out. On March 26, the East Pakistanis declared an independent country named Bangladesh.

3

Pakistani former Prime Minister Benazir Bhutto has been assassinated in a suicide attack.

Ms. Bhutto—the first woman PM [prime minister] in an Islamic state—was leaving an election rally in Rawalpindi when a gunman shot her in the neck and set off a bomb. At least 20 other people died in the attack and several more were injured.

BBC News, Dec. 27, 2007

◀ A BBC report on the assassination of Benazir Bhutto (1953-2007) as she was campaigning for reelection in 2007. She was Pakistan's first woman prime minister (1988-1990 and 1993-1996) and the daughter of Prime Minister Zulfikar Ali Bhutto (1928-1979). A group linked to al-Qa`ida, an Islamist extremist group, claimed responsibility for her death. They condemned her views as pro-Western (favoring the United States and Europe over the Middle East), pro-women's rights, and anti-Taliban [a militant Islamic political group that gained control of most of Afghanistan beginning in the mid-1990's]. Her death was a sign of the disturbance gripping modern Pakistan as Islamists, Western-style democrats, and the military competed for power.

4

▶ Pakistani women express their shock and grief at the 2007 assassination of Benazir Bhutto. The murder was a blow not just for Pakistani democracy but also for all women in a country where liberty was sometimes threatened by Islamic fundamentalism.

NOW YOU KNOW

- Pakistan became an Islamic republic in 1956.
- The country has alternated between civilian and military rule.
- The influence of Islamic militants has grown enormously from the 1990's onward.

Timeline

1498	Vasco da Gama arrived at Kozhikode, Calicut, opening a direct trade route between India and Europe.
1526	The Mughal Dynasty took control of much of India.
early 1600's	The East India Company established an Indian base.
1757	The Battle of Plassey left Britain the dominant European power in India.
1857	The Indian Rebellion, or Sepoy Rebellion, or Indian Mutiny, took place against the East India Company.
1858	The Government of India Act (1858) meant that British government replaced the East India Company as the ruling power in India.
1869	Mohandas Gandhi was born.
1876	*"Vande Mataram,"* Indian national song, was written.
	Mohammad Ali Jinnah was born.
	Queen Victoria was made empress of India.
1885	The first meeting of the Indian National Congress took place.
1889	Jawaharlal Nehru was born.
1904-1905	Viceroy Curzon provoked outrage over his partitioning of Bengal.
1906	The All-India Muslim League was founded.
1909	The Government of India Act (1909) gave some Indians a greater say in government.
1914-1918	Indian troops served worldwide during World War I.
1919	The Rowlatt Acts maintained wartime security measures.
	The Amritsar Massacre took place.
	The Government of India Act (1919), setting up a Central Legislative Assembly, increased Indian participation in government.
1930	Salt March *satyagraha* (nonviolent resistance campaign) took place.
1935	The Government of India Act (1935) further increased Indian participation in government.
1939-1945	Indian troops served worldwide during World War II.
1942	Japanese troops occupied Burma.
	Quit India Movement *satyagraha* took place.
	The Cripps mission offered post-war independence.
1943	Wavell was appointed viceroy.
	The Bengal famine killed between 1 ½ and 3 million people.
1945	The Simla Conference on independence ended in deadlock.
1946	Election results confirmed the Hindu-Muslim divide.
	The plan for an All-India Union came close to acceptance.
	Jinnah's call for a Direct Action Day led to extended violence among Hindu, Muslim, and Sikh communities.
1947	Mountbatten replaced Wavell as viceroy.
	The Government of India Act of 1947 granted independence after one month.
	Violence increased and waves of Hindu, Muslim, and Sikh refugees swept across many regions.
	Boundary commissions worked to separate East and West Pakistan from India.
	Pakistan became an independent Dominion within the British Commonwealth.
	India became an independent Dominion within the British Commonwealth.
1947–1949	India and Pakistan were at war over Kashmir.
1948	Gandhi was assassinated.
1950	India became a republic.
1956	Pakistan became an Islamic republic.
1971	East Pakistan, the former East Bengal, broke away to become the independent Republic of Bangladesh.
1975	Sikkim, the last independent princely state, joined India.

Sources

4–5 Document 2 – Da Gama, Vasco. Description of his landing in India. In *The Library of Original Sources.* Vol. 5. New York: University Research Extension, 1907. *Google Books.* Web. 3 May 2010. Document 4 – Roy, Rammohun. *A Second Conference Between an Advocate and an Opponent of the Practice of Burning Widows Alive.* Calcutta: Baptist Mission Press, 1820. *Google Books.* Web. 3 May 2010.

6–7 Document 2 – Roberts, Fredrick S. *Forty-One Years in India.* Vol. 2. London: R. Bentley, 1897. *Google Books.* Web. 3 May 2010. Document 4 – Hazewell, Charles C. "British India." *Atlantic Monthly* Nov. 1857: 85-93. *Atlantic Online.* Web. 3 May 2010.

8–9 Document 2 – Naoroji, Dadabhai. *Essays, Speeches, Addresses and Writings of the Hon'ble Dadabhai Naoroji.* Bombay: Caxton, 1887. *Google Books.* Web. 3 May 2010. Document 3 – Banerjee, Surendranath. Speech to the Indian National Congress. 1915. In *India's Claim for Home Rule.* Madras: Ganesh, 1917. Print.

10–11 Document 1 – Ahmed Khan, Syed. Lecture delivered at Lucknow. In *Sir Syed Ahmed on the Present State of Indian Politics.* Allahabad: Pioneer Press, 1888. *Google Books.* Web. 3 May 2010. Document 3 – Tilak, Bal Gangadhar. Speech delivered at Calcutta. In *Bal Gangadhar Tilak.* Madras: Ganesh, 1919. *Google Books.* Web. 3 May 2010.

12–13 Document 2 – Chatterjee, Bankim Chandra. "Bande Mataram." Trans. Sri Aurobindo. In Boehmer, Elleke, ed. *Empire Writing: An Anthology of Colonial Literature, 1870-1918.* New York: Oxford, 1998. Print. Document 3 – Gandhi, Mohandas. "Hind Swaraj or Indian Home Rule." 1909. *The Collected Works of Mahatma Gandhi.* Vol. 10. New Delhi: Govt. of India, 1999. *GandhiServe.* Web. 3 May 2010.

14–15 Document 1 – "Home Rule for India." *Times* 3 Jan. 1917: 7. Microfilm. Document 3 – Captain A.V.L.B. Agius. In Macdonald, Lyn. *1914-1918 Voices and Images of the Great War.* London: Michael Joseph, 1988. Print.

16–17 Document 2 – Indian National Congress. Punjab Sub-committee. *Report of the Commissioners Appointed by the Punjab Sub-Committee of the Indian National Congress.* Vol. 1. Lahore: K. Santanam, 1920. *GandhiServe.* Web. 3 May 2010. Document 3 – Churchill, Winston S. Amritsar Massacre speech. In *Winston S. Churchill: His Complete Speeches, 1897-1963.* Ed. Robert Rhodes James. Vol. 3. New York: Chelsea House, 1974. Print.

18–19 Document 2 – Great Britain. Parliament. Joint Committee on Indian Constitutional Reform. *Report on Indian Constitutional Reforms.* London: H.M.S.O., 1918. *Google Books.* Web. 3 May 2010. Document 3 – Gandhi, Mohandas. Letter to the Viceroy, Lord Chelmsford. In *Freedom's Battle.* 2nd ed. Madras: Ganesh, 1922. *Project Gutenberg.* Web. 3 May 2010.

20–21 Document 2 – Gandhi, Mohandas. "Hind Swaraj or Indian Home Rule." In *The Collected Works of Mahatma Gandhi.* Vol. 10. New Delhi: Govt. of India, 1999. *GandhiServe.* Web. 3 May 2010. Document 3 – Gandhi, Mohandas. Letter to Jawaharlal Nehru. In *The Collected Works of Mahatma Gandhi.* Vol. 26.

22–23 Document 1 – Nehru, Jawaharlal. Letter to Dehra Dun prison. 1922. In *A Bunch of Old Letters.* London: Asia Pub. House, 1960. Print. Document 3 – Bose, Subhas Chandra. Letter to Sarat Chandra Bose. 1920. In *The Essential Writings of Netaji Subhas Chandra Bose.* Delhi: Oxford, 1997. Print.

24–25 Document 1 – Nehru, Jawaharlal. Speech to the Congress Party. 27 Dec. 1936. Quoted in *Toward Freedom: The Autobiography of Jawaharlal Nehru.* 1936. Boston: Beacon Press, 1958. Print. Document 3 – Churchill, Winston. Speech to the West Essex Conservative Association. 23 Feb. 1931. In *Never Give In! The Best of Winston Churchill's Speeches.* New York: Hyperion, 2003. Print.

26–27 Document 2 – Jinnah, Mohammad Ali. *The Collected Works of Quaid-e-Azam Mohammad Ali Jinnah.* Comp. Syed Sharifuddin Pirzada. Vol. 2. Karachi: East &West Pub., 1986. Print. Document 3 – Jinnah, Mohammad Ali. Speech given in Lahore. In Ahmad, Jamil-ud-Din, ed. *Some Recent Speeches and Writings of Mr. Jinnah.* Vol. 1. Lahore: S.M. Ashraf, 1943. Print.

28–29 Document 1 – Gandhi, Mohandas. Letter to Adolf Hitler. In *The Collected Works of Mahatma Gandhi.* Vol. 76. New Delhi: Govt. of India, 1999. *GandhiServe.* Web. 3 May 2010. Document

2 – Congress Party. Working Committee report. 1939. In Rajshekhar. *Myanmar's Nationalist Movement (1906-1948) and India.* New Delhi: South Asian Publishers, 2006. Print.

30–31 Document 2 – Bandyopadhyay, Manik. "Why Didn't They Snatch Food to Eat?" *The 1943 Bengal Famine.* Kalpana Bardhan, n.d. Web. 3 May 2010. Document 3 – Wavell, Archibald Percival. Telegram to London. 1943. In *Wavell: The Viceroy's Journal.* London: Oxford, 1973. Print.

32–33 Document 1 – Great Britain. Declaration of the British Government: the Cripps Proposals. In Mishra, Vibhuti Bhushan. *Evolution of the Constitutional History of India, 1773-1947.* Delhi: Mittal, 1987. Print. Document 4 – "Mr. Gandhi Puts His Case to His Party." *Times* 8 Aug. 1942: 4. Microfilm.

34–35 Document 2 – Great Britain. Cabinet Mission to India. *Statement by the Cabinet Mission and His Excellency the Viceroy.* Cmd. 6821. London: H.M.S.O., 1946. Document 3 – Council of the Muslim League. Statement rejecting the Mission Plan. In *Speeches and Documents on the Indian Constitution, 1921-47.* Vol. 2. New York: Oxford, 1957. Print.

36–37 Document 1 – Jinnah, Mohammad Ali. In Wolpert, Stanley. *A New History of India.* 5th ed. New York: Oxford, 1997. Print. Document 2 – "More than 1,000 Dead in Calcutta" *Times* 19 Aug. 1946: 4. Microfilm.

38–39 Document 2 – Wavell, Archibald Percival. Letter to Lord Louis Mountbatten. In Lewin, Ronald. *The Chief: Field Marshall Lord Wavell.* New York: Farrar, Straus, Giroux, 1980. Print. Document 3 – Nehru, Jawaharlal. *Selected Works.* Vol. 2. New Delhi: Jawaharlal Nehru Memorial Fund, 1984. Print.

40–41 Documents 1 and 2– Quoted in Collins, Larry, and Dominique Lapierre. *Freedom at Midnight.* New York: Simon & Schuster, 1975. Print.

42–43 Document 2 – McDougal, Dan. "The Forgotten Refugees Who Wait for Justice After 60 Years." *Observer* 5 Aug. 2007. *Guardian.co.uk.* Web. 3 May 2010. Document 3 – Ahmed, Ishtiaq. "Forced Migration and Ethnic Cleansing in Lahore in 1947." Stockholm University, 15 Jun. 2004. *Swedish South Asian Studies Network.* Web. 3 May 2010.

44–45 Document 2 – Mountbatten, Lord Louis. Letter to Maharaj Rana of Dholpur. In Ziegler, Philip. *Mountbatten.* New York: Knopf, 1985. Print. Document 3 – Khan, Taley Mohammed, Nawab of Palanpur. In French, Patrick. *Liberty or Death.* London: HarperCollins, 1997. Print.

46–47 Document 1 – Singh, Master Tara. Sikh Memorandum to the Cabinet Mission. In *Speeches and Documents on the Indian Constitution, 1921-47.* Vol. 2. New York: Oxford, 1957. Print. Document 2 – Jinnah, Mohammad Ali. In Zakaria, Rafiq. *The Man Who Divided India.* Mumbai: Popular Prakashan, 2001. Print.

48–49 Document 2 – "Partition of India." *Times* 15 Aug. 1947: 5. Microfilm. Document 4 – Collins, Larry, and Dominique Lapierre. *Freedom at Midnight.* New York: Simon & Schuster, 1975. Print.

50–51 Document 2 – Jinnah, Mohammad Ali. Inaugural Address to the Constituent Assembly of Pakistan. In *Voices of Indian Freedom Movement.* Vol. 10. New Delhi: Akashdeep, 1993. Print. Document 4 – "Divided India." *Times* 19 Sept. 1947: 4. Microfilm.

52–53 Document 1 – Singh, Karan. *Heir Apparent.* New York: Oxford, 1982. Document 2 – United Nations. Security Council. *Resolution 38.* UN Doc. S/651. 17 Jan. 1948. Web. 3 May 2010.

54–55 Document 1 – "Assassination of Mr. Gandhi." *Times* 31 Jan. 1948. *TimesOnline.* Web. 3 May 2010. Document 3 – Nehru, Jawaharlal. Speech at New Delhi. 30 Jan. 1948. In *Independence and After.* Freeport, N.Y.: Books for Libraries, 1971. Print.

56–57 Document 1 – Nehru, Jawaharlal. Speech at the Constituent Assembly. 14 Aug. 1947. In *Independence and After.* Freeport, N.Y.: Books for Libraries, 1971. Print. Document 3 – Nayar, Kuldip. "Why Did We Falter?" *Deccan Herald* 16 Aug. 2000. Web. 3 May 2010.

58–59 Document 1 – Pakistan. Ministry of Law. *The Constitution of the Islamic Republic of Pakistan.* Karachi: Govt. of Pakistan, 1956. Print. Document 3 – "Benazir Bhutto Killed in Attack." *BBC News.* 27 Dec. 2007. Web. 3 May 2010.

Additional resources

Books

Benazir Bhutto: Pakistani Prime Minister and Activist, by Mary Englar, Compass Point Books, 2006

Gandhi, by Amy Pastan, DK Publishing, 2006

Gandhi: The Young Protester Who Founded a Nation, by Philip Wilkinson, National Geographic Society, 2005

India (Opposing Viewpoints series), by Jamuna Carroll, Greenhaven Press, 2009

Pakistan, by Samuel W. Crompton, Chelsea House, 2003

Pakistan (Countries in Crisis series), by Alan Wachtel, Rourke Publishing, 2009

Websites

http://news.bbc.co.uk/2/hi/south_asia/country_profiles/1155813.stm
BBC News, a news agency in the United Kingdom, presents a timeline of key events in India from 1858 to the present.

http://news.bbc.co.uk/2/hi/south_asia/country_profiles/1156716.stm
BBC News also presents a timeline of key events in Pakistan from 1906 to the present.

http://english.emory.edu/Bahri/Part.html
A site from Emory University that contains timelines, historical background, and a bibliography on the 1947 partition of India.

http://www.sscnet.ucla.edu/southasia/History/Gandhi/gandhi.html
A collection of articles about Mohandas K. Gandhi, his role in achieving independence for India, and his influence in shaping the nation.

http://www.historytoday.com/ian-talbot/jinnah-and-making-pakistan
A biography of Mohammad Ali Jinnah, the Muslim leader who became known as the founder of Pakistan.

Index

Index

Acknowledgments

AKG-Images: 7 (British Library), 16 (Yvan Travert), 20, 34 (Archiv Peter Rühe), 53, 56 (ullstein bild); **The Art Archive:** 44 (Volkmar K. Wentzel/NGS Image Collection); **Bridgeman Art Library:** 8 (National Army Museum), 17, 18 (Illustrated London News Picture Library), 31 (Private Collection/The Stapleton Collection); **Corbis:** 24 (Hulton-Deutsch Collection), 25, 26, 51, 58 (Bettmann), 59 (Nadeem Khawer/epa); **Dinodia:** 4, 10, 19, 32, 54 (Link); **Getty Images:** 35 (Popperfoto), 23, 47, 55 (Time & Life Pictures), 1, 11, 13, 14, 22, 37, 38, 39, 49, 50; **Kobal:** 57 (DAMFX); **Mary Evans Picture Library:** 42; **Stewart Ross:** 15; **Topfoto:** 5, 12, 29, 30, 33, 41, 48.

Cover main image: **Corbis** (Rahat Dar/epa); inset image: **Getty Images**